John Wesley-Evangelist

Bringing the Church To A Changing World

WORKBOOK

Friendly Visitation Evangelism

Le David Morris

WORKBOOK: Friendly Visitation Evangelism

Published by
Heavenly Herald Books
A Division of DD Images
18 Sanders Rd, Building 2
Humboldt, TN 38343
Phone: 731-499-3815
Website: www.morrislrd.com
Email: morris@click1.net

ISBN: 13:978-0615862361

ISBN: 10:0615862365

PREFACE

What do we ask?

The question should be, "How do we attract a wide variety of non-church people to Jesus Christ?" Are we achieving our mission of seeking and saving the lost as Jesus would? Do we miss the point when our questions focus on filling the pews and adding to congregational rolls?

The response

Maybe the answer to the above questions is evident. The evangelistic outreach is as simple as taking the church to where we find people in our neighborhood. It seems the church's concern should be looking for the lost and bringing them to encounter the living Christ. He went to where people were. He did not seek the powerful or influential. Rather he sought people who needed the saving power and impact of the gospel.

Searching

Perhaps we should discover ways using current tools to engage folks where they are and in context of who they are. Can we be regular and stable in our effort? Maybe the answers are already spread before us in understanding and applying the methods from growing churches.

What we know

I strongly believe many United Methodist Church members are capable of writing a book on friendly visitation evangelism. We understand individual and personal contacts are essential to help churches relate to their community. We spend a tremendous amount of time exploring the intricacies of growing churches. Many study groups focus on some particular aspect of the way to conduct ministry. Advanced study programs explore the subject.

Church Visitation is the culmination of thirty five years of research and study. It began at Memphis Theological Seminary and continues today. I have observed what makes churches reaching out for Christ grow beyond their doors.

Continue to study

Following seminary several young ministers formed a study group to further explore why our denomination was declining. I spent several summers, at the University of South, The School of Theology in their advanced study program, specializing and concentrating on evangelism. The content of the work you are reading started to develop from that study.

The study involved researching many books, journal articles and several doctoral theses in preparing the following work. I want to thank Memphis Theological Seminary, Duke University, and the University of the South for the use of their theological libraries. I would be remiss if I did not acknowledge the instructors at these schools who assisted me in finding crucial information in my journey to uncover the secrets of evangelism.

To those who have read the manuscript found on the pages that produced the book you are reading, I wish to offer my thanks. Lastly, I am indebted to those that helped proofing and editing over and over again.

I do not consider myself an expert on church growth or evangelism. I find the topic hopeful in exploring the possibility to halting decline in my denomination. The following work is developed as a result.

The approach is from one congregation at a time. It works whether you are a small, a mid-size or a large congregation.

The results depend on the amount of effort and enthusiasm you put into the growth of your local church. The material in the ***Workbook*** is drawn from content in the book ***John Wesley-Evangelist***. The main source is Chapter 15 and the reflections at the end of several chapters.

CONTENTS

SECTION ONE
INTRODUCTION

Several years ago a Bible teacher stated, "The way we highlight our Bibles shows our Christian beliefs." He went on to explain that some would mark passages that deal with things like prayer, worship, speaking in tongues, and church attendance.

Then there are those that would underline and mark passages that are concerned with feeding the hungry, clothing the naked, and visiting and ministering to the unchurched. He said some of us gather in our Bible studies, but have no practical application. Some are so busy doing things that they fail to have a relationship with God through Jesus Christ. Concluding again that our discipleship is defined by the scripture verses we mark and use as the motif with which we minister.

It could also be surmised that the writings, theologizing and the exemplification of evangelism is marginally categorized similar to the way one chooses their scripture. Evangelistic theology is so large that in eagerness to prove one's point of view, one may be tempted to give a truncated observation. As a Wesleyan I hope to merge the inward and the outward aspects of the gospel in a holistic approach.

Not only do we separate the gospel, but we change it by omission. We are then confronted to live and participate the whole gospel as the people of God. Evangelism then is the process of presenting the good news where love of God and love of neighbor are the most important aspects of a whole gospel.

Evangelism that focuses on filling the pews misses the mark. In Romans 10 we find that it is the role of the preacher to share the gospel message. If our preaching is limited, then our good news will become limited to the hearer. As a result, we as leaders and evangelists have an awesome task set before us.

Ephesians 4, Romans 12, and I Corinthians 12 express that there is a diversity of gifts, tasks, and ministries, but one God, and from a practical point of view one Gospel message. We are challenged to take the parts we like as well as the parts we prefer to overlook and combine them to create the whole gospel to men, women, boys and girls becoming whole.

Reflective Commentary

We will look at a couple of ideas that may help churches grow. If we see these methods as church growth tools, without the Biblical base of bringing people to a relationship with Jesus Christ, we will get discouraged and fail. When we focus on expanding God's message the chances multiply that God will grant increase.

There is a secret that Jesus demonstrated and was exhibited by John Wesley and the Holy Club. Later on Mr. Wesley adapted the secret wherever he went to spread the gospel message. You will find a hint of this as we progress through the writing of ***Church Visitation***.

Questions

What is the most important aspect of Bible study?

_____

_____

_____

Is there one particular approach to Bible study?

_____

_____

Does the Bible provide insight to the way we live today?
Why?

_____

_____

SECTION TWO

The following contain common threads that provide the secret to church growth throughout the last 2100 years.

A Fresh Beginning

Andrews Chapel has been in existence for 120 years. The members of the church decided to close at Annual Conference June, 2013. The congregation had been in decline and not able to afford repairs and upkeep needed to maintain the church and grounds. The situation came to the notice of Rev. Dan Camp, pastor of First United Methodist Church in Jackson, Tennessee.

Rev. Camp presented the dilemma to the congregation of his church to determine if they could help the remaining church members at Andrews Chapel UMC. The response was tremendous. The trustee board at First

United Methodist, in agreement with the small congregation of Andrews Chapel, decided to assume the property at the end of Annual Conference from the conference trustees. It was decided to send part of its staff and volunteers to Andrews Chapel to offer a continuing ministry at the Andrews Chapel Campus.

First United Methodist paid to replace the heating and air conditioning system. They would send different Sunday School classes to attend Andrews Chapel during July, 2013 and provide follow-up visitation into the community starting in August. Groups of workers volunteered to spruce up the grounds and properties.

July 7, 2013 was the date that First UMC began sending someone to preach at the morning worship. The attendance was 147. The next two Sundays it hovered around sixty.

Question

What other solution might be a possibility?

Moscow UMC

Moscow United Methodist Church takes the charge of friendly visitation evangelism very earnestly.

The Rev. James Graham, the pastor, shared that Moscow UMC at Moscow Tennessee has a growing friendship with their new Hispanic neighbors. It began when one of his church members stated that God desired that their church needed to invite the Hispanics to worship them.

Rev. Graham informed the parishioner that he hadn't seen any Hispanic neighbors in the community. The parishioner claimed that they were close to the church.

Graham called his Hispanic speaking friend David Salas, and they decided together that God was leading them into a new ministry.

The Hispanic ministry started in the 2013 year. The new ministry began with knocking on doors and inviting new people to a fresh multi-language service. The service was conducted at the Moscow United Methodist Church. As of June, 2013, 17 Hispanics are worshiping at the Moscow UMC.

Hispanics living close to the Moscow church are developing an ongoing relationship through ministry. Additionally, they have become a part of the church community. A festival was celebrated at the on Cinco de Mayo. It was a great success.

Pastor Graham has reported the establishment of classes in English as a second language using the church's facilities.

David Salas and his wife, Eleanor, have united with the Moscow church. At present they conduct services in Spanish and English. Their hopes are to eventually combine the services.

Graham and Silas look to God for direction as to where the ministry will lead them. Their expectations in the future are that language will not be a barrier.

Question

How would you approach the situation?

FIRST GRACE UMC

The writer of ***Church Visitation*** discovered First Grace United Methodist Church of New Orleans in October, 2011. They represent the best display of cooperative effort in mission and ministry. The writer was on a study tour to discover how to develop Hispanic Ministries and friendly visitation evangelism. First Grace qualified in both arenas.

They visited house to house in their neighborhood inviting their new friends to experience Christ through the work of their church regardless of race or ethnic origin.

Two United Methodist churches, less than one mile apart, came together to form a new church on October 21, 2007 as a result of Hurricane Katrina. First UMC, a white congregation and Grace UMC, a black congregation, combined to form First Grace UMC.

In their first year together, the worshiping churches went from 60 members to more than 130. Additionally, a Hispanic/Latino ministry joined First Grace. The Latino/Hispanic population has been steadily growing. First Grace reflects the diverse residents of New Orleans.

Through visiting in the community the Hispanic participation increased. The need for English as a second language began to surface. The Hispanic membership continued to grow until a third service conducted in Spanish emerged. A Spanish speaking minister was secured for the service.

They celebrate their unique diversity. As the body of Christ their choice of working together in New Orleans was viewed as courageous. They engage the city's population through worship, mission and through serving meals on Sundays. They provide meals from their food pantry for people in need. They shelter women and children at Hagar's House, having Wednesday night Pot Luck and Community Bible Study, an Orgacni Community Garden and various other ministries.

The church joined with the New Orleans Faith Health Alliance, the March of Dimes mother/baby bus, Elba Medical and the New Orleans Workers' Center for Racial Justice. These associations provide health care for the working uninsured, free vaccinations for infants, needed prenatal care for expectant mothers, and help workers across ethnic lines to find jobs in Post-Katrina New Orleans.

They want visitors and residents to feel welcomed and moved by the loving Gospel of Jesus Christ that lights our path. They are continuing to repair the structure from the five feet of flood water that eroded the facilities.

Question

Would you feel comfortable in such a diverse group?

_____

_____

Loved and Overlooked

The writer of **_Church Visitation_** loves and appreciates the United Methodist Church. Often those that love the institution can overlook its failings, or we can excuse it in many ways. We want the best for the church, but may not know how to overcome the years of decline. We do not solve our problems by pointing our fingers at specific problems and blaming others. If we can recognize who we are and approach our problems as instruction tools we may be able to overcome our deficits in positive ways. However, there is new growth springing up all over the country.

Perhaps the answer can be undertaken by the denomination, or maybe it might boil down to exploring opportunities for growth on an individual congregational basis church by church. Population has shifted from rural and urban America to suburban areas.

Look at the questions spread throughout the **_Workbook_**. They may give us an indication of how far we need to regroup around Wesley's precepts.

Question

Do we overlook "things" that need to be accomplished because we are used to the way "things" are?

Do not give up

Several years ago in the urban area of a large metropolitan city a church was gradually declining. One student minister said, "let us start a friendly visitation program visiting from house to house in the community. The adults claimed it would not work, because they had done that before. It was too much work for the effort.

He did not give up. However, he approached the youth of the church with an idea. He even suggested that there would be a pizza party afterwards. The night was arranged, and two person teams were chosen. After a brief training on listening and not talking they were sent off with an encouraging prayer.

After the visitation was over the kids reported that they had encountered many nice people. Overall, twenty families claimed they would be at church Sunday morning.

When Sunday came there were eight visiting families for a total of 21 people including adults and children. A buzz surrounded the church. The church continued visitation with youth and adults for several months until their student minister was reassigned to another appointment.

Their new minister did not continue the visitation emphasis. The church started declining again and has closed. Some of the former members said we wonder if we would have continued to visit house to house would we still be a viable church.

The community was changing ethnically and racially. Many were afraid to embrace the new residents. Not much was said, but suspicion was rampant. The majority of the residents fled in droves. Others moved in taking advantage of low housing costs.

Question

Would continuing visitation have helped this church to grow? What would you do?

Snellville UMC

Snellville United Methodist Church of the North Georgia Conference began inviting the new Hispanic residents in their community to come to their church several years ago. The Hispanic portion of the congregation grew to over 100 attendees. The Hispanic members of the congregation said a separate afternoon worship service in Spanish would be beneficial.

The pastor agreed. A local pastor emerged to conduct the services in Spanish. The Hispanic members and attendees continued to increase to the point that Snellville UMC bought the former city hall building next door to house the Hispanic ministry. Today the Hispanic attendees number in excess of 200 and members are encouraged to choose to attend either the services conducted in English or Spanish.

Question

What other solutions should a church in this situation explore?

_____

_____

A sad example

A young United Methodist minister and his wife were attending an advanced study program in a neighboring area of a different annual conference. The little church they visited was cold and uninviting. No one welcomed them. No one invited them to stay for Sunday School. No one offered to show them where the rest rooms were or any part of the facilities.

After the couple were seated two older ladies came to where they were seated and informed them in an angry manner that they were seated in their pews. The couple were told them they needed to move.

Needless to say the young couple did not return, even though the advanced study program lasted all summer long. The church was the closest congregation of their denomination. This was a new experience – feeling totally unwelcomed in their own denomination.

They did find other nearby churches that were open and presented a friendly inviting atmosphere where they felt at home away from home.

Question

Do we need to train our congregation to be open and friendly to visitors?

_____

_____

New hope

With advocates like Bob Farr and David Platt we may discover the answer to reversing our decline and reexamining ourselves in the mode of evangelism. Thomas C. Oden needs attention as he presents his four volume work ***John Wesley Teachings***.[1]

John Wesley's ministry was directed to bringing the lost in his day to the church and to confront having a relationship with God through Jesus Christ. He went to where people were. As mentioned previously he did not seek the ones of power and influence. He sought those who needed the saving impact of the gospel. Do we need to look at ways to meet people where they are today? Are there things that we should do with persistent diligence?

---

[1]   Thomas C. Oden, ***John Wesley Teachings, Vol. I-IV***, (Grand Rapids, Zondervan, 2012-2013.)

Question

Does Jesus call us to visit strangers?

_____

_____

Inventory

We know that saying that our churches are open for all to come in is not the answer. It may satisfy us that we are doing something, but are we really? Do we need to answer the questions throughout the workbook and be guided to action?

Questions

What methods can and should you use to connect with people for Christ?

_____

How do you help people come to your church?

The above questions are not directed at nor an indictment toward the church. They are talking points to consider when devising plans for implementing and growing churches.

I have discovered and encountered over 2,000 new contacts, connections or friends working around 20 minutes a day on Facebook, LinkedIn and Google+. My experiment lasted about five weeks. The key is just be friendly. Do not be obnoxious or pushy. Just accept people where they are and help them to become better.

SECTION THREE

Twelve Essential Elements to Elevate Eminent Exultation --

An Enlightenment

The month of October, 2011 was a time spent studying why a few churches were growing and other churches were not. To my surprise it was discovered that the growing churches had a common element. There were some accompanying factors, but the primary reason was in the simplicity of creating a visitation outreach. The 27 churches that were studied were mostly in the Southeast Jurisdiction, except for two churches in Arkansas and one church in Indiana. The research was cursory, but deep enough to disclose that in some way each of these congregations ventured out into their communities to invite their neighbors to church.

Some did the invitation process on a short term basis. However, the most successful churches did the inviting as an ongoing process of visitation evangelism. Some found and invited ethnic groups that were different than the primary make up of their membership, some did not.

The churches were small, medium and large congregations. The motivation was to reach others in their community for Jesus Christ, with the exception of one. Details follow --

Bethel UMC

Bethel United Methodist Church had gotten to the point that they could not replace their antiquated heating/air conditioning system with the 20 members remaining in their congregation.

In January they approached their District Superintendent about closing the church. They came to a conclusion that they could hold on until spring, but not any longer.

What happened next was an amazing feat. The remaining members decided to go out with a celebration of the gloriousness that the church had meant in the past. They began writing former members and friends inviting them to come and celebrate the memory of times past as participants in the homecoming and the closing of the Bethel church.

Someone suggested that they invite their neighbors in the community to share the special time. They went out into the rural area with a friendly inviting attitude to come celebrate with us the past as we have our final services. There was a very positive approach in their invitation.

When the day of celebration arrived there were over one hundred in attendance. A consensus emerged that the attendees did not want to let Bethel church close.

Someone made a suggestion that a special offering be taken to facilitate purchasing a new heating/cooling system. Volunteers said they would make the needed repairs. Others said they would come and make the church their church home. To shorten the story, Bethel is flourishing today. It did not close its doors and it has a bright future.

Question

Are there other churches that need to recapture their excitement and enthusiastic outreach for Christ?

_____

_____

Elusiveness

The secret to evangelism in the church is not a secret at all. It was practiced by Wesley, then by his lay preachers and exemplified by Francis Asbury. It was practiced in the class meetings, and by the bands. It was a natural progression as Methodists moved across the face of the United States.

Some way we have forgotten its thrust. We may have gotten so educated and sophisticated that we can not remember why we did it originally. We have gotten busy and bogged down with other concerns. Time constraints prevent us from looking at this simple methodology for church growth.

In the scheme of things we often find ourselves in a similar situation to Saul son of Kish. Saul was about to be publicly recognized by the prophet Samuel as the first king of Israel. He could not be found. He was hiding among the stuff (baggage). The question then, "do we hide among the stuff in such a way that we are doing things that keeps us from doing the most important things that God calls us to do?"(See 1 Samuel 10:20 ff.)

Then what is it that God calls us to do? What prevents us from understanding? It was so dynamic that it changed the religious outlook of the world and most importantly in England under John Wesley and Francis Asbury in America.

A summation of the message focuses on the essence of this non-secret. Wesley went to where hurting and needful people were. He compelled them to come to church and invited them to hear the word of God delivered by Methodist preachers and speakers. Basically he issued a friendly and loving invitation to visit.

Let it be said again. The chief method that John Wesley used was going to where people were and inviting them to come to church for communion, and to come to hear the word of God from the Methodists. What a concept! We know Wesley was immolating what Jesus did, as he went from place to place presenting the gospel message in many forms. He sent his preannouncers to herald his coming to particular areas to preach.

It is not the purpose of the author to claim that friendly visitation evangelism is the only solution to church growth, but it is often overlooked because other important things seem to take priority. Thus, friendly visiting is simply one method to enhance the possibility that someone will encounter Christ.

Question

How can friendly visitation evangelism help your church grow?

_____

_____

Emerging Exposure

The essentials to Wesley were helping people discover Christ through any method necessary. We today may find this a difficult job in the American church. I concede that many have not widely practiced friendly visitation evangelism in recent years. The lives of our churches depend on it. Churches that are growing have established some sort of friendly community visitation program. They view it as part of their call to ministry or evangelism, and part of their strategy to grow churches.

Charles Wesley was innovative in integrating familiar music to his Christian words, phrases and poetry. Today we need to be careful that we do not infringe on copyright laws. Many people feel comfortable with certain styles or types of music while others are open to a variety of presentations. There are those that get upset when we stray from the traditional worship services.

Experience of listening to former unchurched and lightly churched members in growing churches suggest moderate changes. They receive a sense of joy and excitement when presented with non-traditional methods of using words flashing on projected screens. Churches that focus on the unchurched keep their priorities in order and their goals in clear view.

Many growing churches add projection screens and new music in addition to maintaining traditional hymnbooks gradually to make it easier for established members to accept. The essential element to keep in mind is what it will take to incorporate new visitors into a Christian relationship and membership within the church.

Question

What can we do to demonstrate friendliness in our church?

_____

_____

Embracing

Many of us think that friendly visitation is something we do every once in a while. God calls us to ministry. It is a shame that most churches relegate friendly and loving visitation as an afterthought. We need to reprioritize our thoughts and efforts.

Churches do not grow or decline by one factor, but those without friendly visitation as part of their evangelistic outreach seem to be the most open to decline. We must appeal to those outside our immediate congregations with a magnetic draw. If our plea is nothing more than a ploy to fill the pews, we are grossly misdirected.

We must have a heart for reaching the unchurched for Christ. What greater place to start than in our own back yard or front yard! Our desire must be to bring people to Christ in our community. We must develop relationships with those outside the church. We require a consideration of importance for mission and ministry. There are several new churches in most communities that make evangelism their essential effort. I am afraid to say that not many are United Methodist. The key to evangelism is friendly visitation.

Exciting events

Hold special exciting events annually like homecoming, youth day, women's day or men's day, to name a few. Space out special events on a quarterly basis. Have a monthly event to celebrate birthdays and anniversaries. Invite guest speakers, revival ministers and missionaries to present programs. Host a gospel singing group. Do book studies and training events. Do anything where excitement can be created.

Whatever you do build enthusiasm and excitement into the event. Do not just have a Vacation Bible School. Have a secret treasure hunt or a Bible camp centered around a particular Bible character or personality. Cluster with two or three churches for your special program.

Keep a variety of activities going. Overstate and promote your activities. Put out fliers and posters advertising your events. Invite the community.

SECTION FOUR
Explainable

There are many that understand the "how to" of church growth and evangelism. They can give you many details of all the correct ways to make churches grow. We often miss that the most important aspect is not the "how to" do it, but "why do" we do it.

Wesley was transparent in the why – even some of the writers in the church growth movement of thirty years ago presented the why in a plain manner. Those of us that read their material and those of us that even studied Wesley in an in-depth manner often overlooked the why and opted for the how to.

Instilled in the gospel message itself is a mandate of the why. Every sermon should be directed toward the why, as well as every piece of Christian literature and writing. The why is what binds it all together.

The why focuses our thoughts on the love of God and the relationship we have with God. Wesley discovered that many did not have a relationship with God and directed his mission and ministry toward helping others find God through Jesus Christ. Establishing the why motivated Wesley's purpose and propelled him on his lifelong work.

Any attempt at friendly visitation evangelism without the motivation to bring people to a loving relationship with God is misdirected. Salvation and discipleship becomes the goal and evangelism is the means or process.

Exploration

Friendly visitation is exploration. Initially it helps uncover who are churched and unchurched and to invite them to church. It is not the job of the visitation team to lead someone to salvation unless the visitor is gifted in that area. It is the primary function to invite and encourage those visited to come to church.

Whether we admit it or not we all have things that are greater than our ability with which to deal. At times we need God's intervention. While visitors are at church do we help them find a solution through Jesus Christ? The unchurched are seeking solutions and often find them through up-to-date biblical teaching and preaching. If the teaching and preaching fall short the probability of them remaining will be short lived.

Emphasize

It is not the job of the pastor to do the work of visitation evangelism. He/she may or may not have a role of leadership in the process. He/she may or may not be gifted in the area of visitation. However, it is important that the pastor embrace the concept and provide training and direction for incorporating the visitation program within the church. Thus, the pastor can make it happen and is the key to it happening within the congregation. Without pastoral support visitation will die.

Any pastor has limited time to devote to ministry including preaching, teaching, and visiting. Priorities of the pastor's time is an important consideration. Congregations that fail to realize that will debilitate a pastor's ministry. Pastors that fail to realize it will find themselves lacking or burned out.

Questions

What are you as a church doing to reach people for Christ?

_____

What are you as an individual doing to reach people for Christ?

_____

How often do you contact someone new for Christ?

_____

Enthusiasm and Excitement

Have those doing the visitation look at themselves in the mirror and smile. It may sound silly, but a forced smile with pleasant thoughts will evoke a real smile. Keeping pleasant thoughts in your mind will assist in maintaining a smile that is both evident and natural.

Churches need to be uplifting and friendly. All church members must be congenial. A simple smile or encouraging comment demonstrates sincerity and authentic interest. Most churches believe they are friendly. Only when we show it by our actions are we believed. Even the way we relate to others is observed by visitors.

If we love others it will show through. We show who we are publically. We must exhibit the best that Christ has to offer us. Outsiders have lofty regard for churches. We affirm or discount our Christian beliefs by our words and actions.

We can find supporting scripture in many places, but maybe the best is found in Acts 5:42 where we find, "Day after day, in the temple courts and from house to house, they never stopped teaching and proclaiming the good news that Jesus is the Christ."

Exhibit the Edifice Excellently

Another issue - Does the church provide a neat, clean and presentable building, especially the bathrooms and the nursery? How would an outsider view the church plant meeting their temporal needs? What a member or insider may miss, because they love their church, "Is the building and grounds fallen to disrepair?"

It speaks loudly to outsiders that the church does not care. We must realize that a visitor will not come back if the property is lacking. We must maintain the building and grounds in all areas in order to attract others to our church.

Elucidate the Location

Does our signage tell who we are? Do we have direction signs strategically placed guiding those looking for our church? Are our signs up to date and inviting? What we say or do speaks loudly about who we are. We need to be knowledgeable about our beliefs and overall ministry and mission.

We know our reason to exist as a church and what we are asking others to believe. Visitors know that they will be asked or encouraged to join in the ongoing activities and anticipate getting involved in the ministry of the church. Make sure it is something substantial. Otherwise they will lose interest. Perhaps evangelistic outreach would be a good place to start.

It is sad to say, but some churches do not want new members. They are very happy with who comes. Any visitor is viewed as the enemy. They have become a closed club - a church in name only. They can not see past the lifespan of their current membership. The love of God and the love of neighbor is missing from who they are. Before you condemn them, it is easy to fall into their trap.

It takes a tough reminder from God to focus our attention beyond ourselves. We have to remind ourselves that we are Jesus' spokespersons in an unchurched world. We hold up the light of Jesus in a dark time.

Questions

When and where can we encounter men, women, boys and girls for Christ?

_____

What mission and ministry are we extending to those outside the walls of our churches?

_____

Have we become so complacent in our middle class and affluent life styles that we believe it is either the pastor's job or a hired visitation specialist to do our visitation evangelism?

_____

Emissaries outside and inside

Do we have someone at the door or even in the parking lot, as well as in the church, prepared to welcome and greet visitors? They can help the visitor get oriented to building locations of restrooms, classrooms, nursery and break rooms. An information center for larger churches will be a big help. Use welcoming persons and greeters from various age ranges. Train them to smile and to be upbeat and helpful.

Questions

How do you attract new people to Christ?

_____

Do we miss opportunities to meet people for Christ?

_____

Do we see ourselves as too old or too comfortable to do the things necessary to reach others for Jesus Christ?

Establish Enlistment

We need to help the visitor find others with whom to bond. Direct them to groups or classes that are prepared to receive them. The groups or classes must be prepared to answer questions and present the biblical message in a non-threatening way. They need to be prepared to help others form friendships.

Small groups and classes powerfully influence a church's incorporation of visitors. Bible study is one avenue for small groups. Child care is another option for small groups. Many churches are not prepared for small group ministries. Wesley did this with bands and classes.

Evoke Empowered Essence

In visiting do not underestimate the power and purpose of prayer. There are two reasons - First, we need the assurance of prayer.

Second, those visited need to experience the power of prayer. Prayer before and during the visitation is necessary. We find healing and acceptance in prayer. We find forgiveness and love in prayer. Prayer proves the way for hope and divine guidance.

On a prayerful note the author hopes the writing will be beneficial to you and others in developing a friendly visitation program.

www.ingramcontent.com/pod-product-compliance
Lightning Source LLC
Chambersburg PA
CBHW081231020426

42331CB00012B/3131